The Plan

Harry Noble

ISBN: 1453671099
ISBN-13: 9781453671092
Library of Congress Control Number: 2010909714

I dedicate this book to my daughter, Landrey.

Contents

Introduction

I'm writing this book because along the way to becoming a successful businessperson, I was constantly asked how I did it. Therefore, I decided to put down on paper a plan for high school seniors, college graduates, and young adults who feel lost when they finish school or don't know quite were to start. By creating a plan and following that plan, you will be surprised how successful your future will become.

Who wants to be a millionaire? I bet if you ask a room of one hundred people, all one hundred would raise their hands. But how are you going to get there? This book will show you how to get there. Use this book as your personal handbook or CliffsNotes to amassing $1 million and more.

No matter what level of education you achieve or how old you are, you can reach your dreams by following your plan! You learn all about theory from elementary to high school and throughout college. But who will teach you application? This book will teach you the plan you will need to apply yourself.

This book is geared toward the application process. Theory is what you will learn in all phases of your education years. But no school that I am aware of will teach you the application process. It takes 90 percent ambition and 10 percent brainpower to follow your plan.

I'm sure you have heard the expression "if you snooze you lose." Well when you reach thirty years of age, you had better be prepared to lay out your goals and plan of attack.

Part I
Education and Passion

The first thing you need is passion. Go ahead and get your high school education and college education because it's a good training ground for the general education you will need to be successful. While you are attending college, and if you are in a school of business, it would be a good idea to take the courses needed to sit for your real estate broker's license. Once you start purchasing property, it will help you understand the terminology and help you save on real estate commissions. It will also look good on your resume and help with financing, which we will get into later.

But, without passion, you will not reach your dream and you will ultimately fall into the "average" category. The younger you are, the more drive and passion you will likely have. Therefore, the sooner you get started, the better. Although you may start at any age, a younger person definitely has the advantage because of the energy and stamina.

Part 2
Experience

Experience, experience, experience is what you must obtain next, no matter what profession you choose. You must spend the next eight to ten years mastering your craft and be the best in that field—in other words, an expert. Yes, an expert—that's what I said—and with focus you can do it.

The years will go by quickly and you will need to make personal sacrifices. What I mean by that is long hours; time away from your family; working weekends, late at night, and early in the morning; and staying focused and being on a mission to succeed! This should be your mantra.

Once you master your craft or profession, you can rely on the cookie-cutter business model you establish; each time you do it, the process will become better and better and easier and easier.

Once you get out of college, you need to go into a business or job that interests you. I remember seeing a man who was a major fast food franchisee and he was driving a Mercedes-Benz. At the time, I thought to myself, *I can do that; he is no smarter than I am and, in fact, I think I can do it better.*

When I got out of college, I went to work as a manager of a steak house in partnership with my father. I learned everything I could about the food industry. How to minimize labor, order inventory, manage all the costs, hire employees, train employees, and so on.

Before you start out on your own business venture, consider the following guidelines/requirements:

1. Be around thirty years old before you go after your first loan, because the loan officer will not take you seriously.
2. Have at least eight to ten years' experience in the profession you decide to tackle.
3. At a minimum, own your own house as collateral. This is what you will need to get your project off the ground.

Part 3
Begin Career Steps

GOALS AND PLAN

Now, I know what you're thinking, *I have worked for the last ten years and own a house, and now you say to give it up as collateral for my first business loan?*

That's exactly what you're going to do. If you fail, it's OK and you will have time to recover because you're only thirty years old. When you are in your fifties, there's no way you can do something like this.

Regardless of your age, you must have clear goals. Now get out a piece of paper and write down a few goals that you want to accomplish. There's no way you are going to get there without looking at these goals every day. Make sure you put them in a place where you can see them, every day.

For instance, when I first started my own plan, I wrote down that I wanted to own at least five fast-food restaurants in three years.

It looked like this: "Build five restaurants in three years." That's the only goal I put in my face every day.

Once you have written your goals, you need to reward yourself with something if you reach your goal. My reward was buying a new, expensive car. I bought a new Cadillac at the end of three years. I did it and you can too.

Remember, I will profess that I'm not the smartest person in the room and you don't have to be either, but you have to be willing to work hard and spend the time and hours needed to get the job done. It will require working weekends and holidays, when everyone else is off. I will admit, however, that what my family said to me was true: "All work and no play will make Jack a dull boy." The first five to eight years, I worked my tail off, but after that, if you looked back and compared my financial well-being to those who criticized me, you would see that my net worth was ten to twenty times, more and I owned real estate, which I controlled and which paid me rent.

This is how you will accumulate wealth through real estate, but you will need a vehicle to get you there. Mine was fast food.

PLAN, PLAN, PLAN

You need a plan. Probably, the best thing I learned in college was the acronym POSDC: the ability to Plan, Organize, Staff, Direct, and Control.

You will need POSDC also; it's just a simple managing tool that every university teaches, but probably the only one you will ever use.

These few words will be your battle cry. Whenever you are not sure how to get started use these words, and before you start any project use these words. Plan, plan, plan!

Then plan for the worst thing that could happen financially. Taking the few minutes to do this will save your ass.

Now let's look back at the "passion" you will need to get started.

You need to know everything about your topic and field, and now it better than anyone else around you. In other words, you need to be an expert in your field of business, whatever it is you decide to do. Be number one in your area of expertise. No one will remember who number two, twenty-nine, or fifty are, but people will remember the best. It's just like the Super Bowl in football. Everyone will remember who won the Super Bowl, but ask them a few months later who they played, and I bet they can't remember.

FIND THE VOID IN THE MARKET

During this eight- to ten-year period, you will need to keep your head out of the sand and see what voids you can fill in your existing local market. No matter where you live, there will always be a void to fill.

The void I found was a lack of Burger King restaurants in my local and surrounding communities. I applied for a franchise and Burger King Corporation told me that I had a seven-year waiting list. I was persistent and applied anyway. Several months and numerous phone calls later, Burger King Corporation invited me to Atlanta for an interview. A few weeks later, they invited me to become a franchisee. Persistence Pays!

A personal note is needed at this time: don't listen to the naysayers. When I opened my first business, everyone told me that the economy was bad, there weren't any good employees out there, and other negative things.

Actually, the best time to start a new business is when the economy is bad. On the banking side, the interest rates are usually low and banks want to make good loans. If you are buying real estate, land prices are generally soft and the construction contractors are very competitive while trying to secure projects to keep their subcontractors working.

All in all, it's a great time to begin your path to financial success and wealth.

ATTACK, ATTACK, ATTACK

Now that you have the passion, the experience, and found the void in the market, attack, attack, attack!

MULTIPLE LOCATIONS

No matter what profession or business you open, the vehicle to get you to financial freedom and more time with your family will be opening multiple locations.

As I mentioned previously, when I opened my first Burger King franchise the corporation made me lease the first location, and that was fine. But when I got ready to open the second Burger King, I bought the real estate for myself.

Now, let's take a closer look at what happened. I leased the first store's location, but for the second store, I bought the real estate and leased it back to myself as a passive investment. What's a passive investment, you ask?

Well, while I paid off the real estate portion of the new Burger King that I built, I also owned and operated the franchise business. My focus was operating the Burger Kings and being the best operator in the system. Instead of leasing the land and building from someone else, I bought it myself and paid rent to, you guessed it, myself. I made sure the rent payment was enough to cover the note payment and voila…a passive investment.

While I was personally spending all my time running the Burger King operations, I was also creating wealth by owning the real estate underneath. I had two corporations. One owned the equipment and the franchise and the other was my properties corporation.

Once the real estate was paid for, the rent from the operations continued to come in and create wealth. In addition, over the course of ten to fifteen years the value of the real estate went up as well.

As I mentioned earlier, once you start cookie-cutter multiple locations, you get wealthier and wealthier, and have more time for your family or whatever your personal interests are.

Most people in this country are wealthy because they own real estate. Therefore, as I said, no matter what profession you decide to go into, real estate will be the underlying vehicle to create a tremendous amount of financial freedom for you. I did it with a fast-food concept, but you can do it with most any profession you choose—the key being multiple locations.

Another key aspect of multiple locations is that it diversifies your risks. Remember the old saying, "Do not put all your eggs in one basket"? When you have multiple locations and all the locations are doing well, then it's great, but when one town or location is doing poorly, having multiple locations helps because they can balance each other out. The economy in all your towns/locations is different; it's just like owning stocks and bonds. Some of your investments will do better than others. Therefore, having multiple locations will lower your risk.

Now, if you do this ten to twenty times, let's see what you will have at the end of the day—one location is leased, but for the rest, you own the real estate and pay rent to yourself. All the while, you maintain the operations of the ten to twenty locations and the profits from that business also. Remember, the real estate is a passive investment, but in the long run will generate twenty times the value and provide more security than you have ever dreamed of having.

Part 4
Wheel of Success

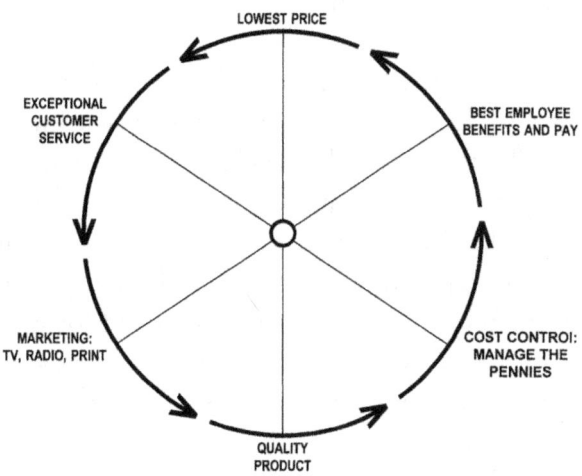

A wheel has a lot of spokes on it and all the items need to be maintained continuously. Now get on the bike and ride this wheel to success!

BEING THE BEST IN YOUR TOWN

As I have mentioned, you have to be the best, or an expert, at what you do, no matter where your career or profession takes you. I remember what a fellow manager said to me one day in my first Burger King restaurant: "You have an answer for everything." That's right, and you better also. Now, if you don't know the answer, let them know you don't know but will get back to them promptly.

I used to play a game in my restaurant with my managers and crew. I would ask questions such as:

How many buns are in a pillow pack?

How many medium Cokes can you get from a gallon of Coke?

How many pickles are in a pickle bucket?

I would constantly ask questions; and slowly but surely, everyone would know the answers and they became experts themselves. The more knowledgeable my crew was, the more successful my business became.

Also, I would give out weekly tests for crew and managers. When they had taken them all, we would repeat the process until everyone knew the material backward and forward.

I also believed in cross-training everyone for every position. The more proficient my crew became, the better the service and higher the standards.

When you have slow time—train, train, train. How many times have you heard how boring work can be? This will help eliminate that problem.

I used to keep a proficiency chart in my restaurant, and this would allow me to follow up on what positions each crew person could perform and where I needed to provide additional training. Just knowing the capabilities of each person was a tremendous help with crew scheduling.

I would like to point out that you should always set high standards for your employees. The higher the better, because usually they will meet you halfway.

Your pricing compared to the competition:

You should never allow your competition to out price you for a similar product or service. Believe me; volume cures a lot of ills. You cannot bank percentages, only dollars. Sometimes, people get caught up in how profitable they are or how low their cost of goods is, but without those dollars in the bank, it's hard to make payroll.

Never, never, never allow your competition to under price you for a similar product or service.

I don't like to use the words never and always, but never make the mistake of being higher on a similar product, no matter what product or profession you are selling.

I used to say, "I want my customers to expect low prices like Wal-Mart and service like IBM." When you give the best price and the best service, you are going to be very successful and deliver high volume to your business.

One bad experience and people will tell ten others, but if you go the extra mile to correct it, you can reverse a bad situation.

You can count on your customers telling everyone in town how great you are if you deliver and exceed their expectations.

Most, or almost all, companies are complacent, and if you control the price and service, you will win the war with your competition.

Also, it's a good idea to price shop monthly to be sure you are staying competitive, then give your customers the best price and service in town, and be proud of it. I say that because when I first started in the restaurant business, people would ask me what I did for a living. I would say I manage a restaurant. Of course, they would respond something like, "Oh, you flip burgers for a living." And I would reply proudly, "I manage a $1,000,000 business every day; what do you do for a living?"

Part 5
How to build the Best Company on Earth

DEVELOP A MISSION STATEMENT

Every company needs to have a mission statement about what the company stands for. For example, when I operated Burger King restaurants, our mission statement was: *To ensure customer satisfaction by consistently delivering the best Quality, Service, and Cleanliness to each and every customer.*

CREATE AN ORGANIZATIONAL CHART

To perform better and clarify the structure of the company, develop an organizational chart so that you can actually see the flow of who reports to whom and who supervises whom.

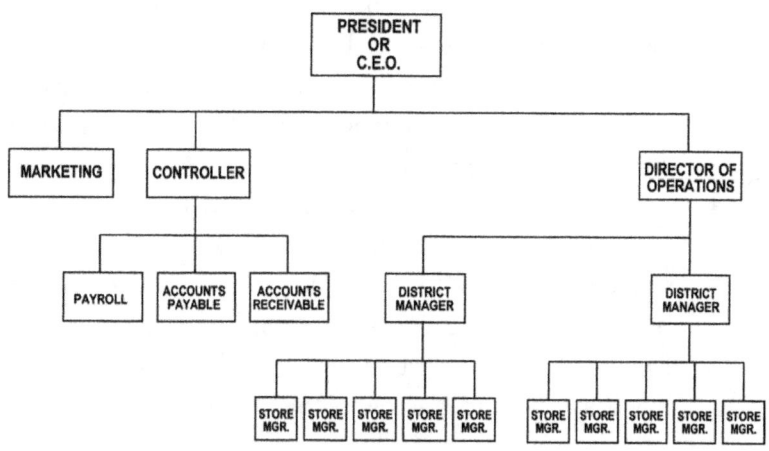

OBTAINING FINANCING

Your first meeting with the banker for a commercial loan will be critical. Needless to say, you will need to look the part also, that is, wear a tie, nice slacks, a jacket, and so on. One day, you will look back and realize that you make ten times more money that the guy you got the loan from, but for now you have to be humble and beg.

Yes, I did say that—I mean beg. I used to kid that when I was going out to secure money for my next restaurant that I had to put my kneepads on!

Here are some fine points to consider when dealing with the bank or lender

- Always be sure that you have no prepayment penalties in the loan. You need this in case you want to pay off the loan early or change lenders at some point.
- Be sure and set some ceilings and floors on the rate if you use a floating rate. For instance, if your rate is based on the ten-year Treasury, it might look something like this: The rate is 250 to 350 basis points above the ten-year Treasury, with a ceiling of 100 points above and below. So if the ten-year Treasury interest rate is 3.25 currently, then your rate would be 5.75 and adjusted quarterly, if the rate changes. In other words, the rate could not go higher than 6.75 or lower than 4.75.
- Most of the time, I personally asked for the "prime rate" and borrowed at prime plus 1.00 when I first got started, with a ceiling and floor of 1.5 up or down. But after I built up a good relationship with my lender, I requested to convert to prime, and before I sold my business, I would borrow below prime.

- It's also a good idea to borrow from several lenders in the beginning.
- Schedule the dates the payments are due, such as the fifth, tenth, fifteenth, twentieth, and twenty-fifth of the month, to a convenient and doable payment schedule for your income, especially if you have multiple notes.
- Typically, banks prefer floating rates versus fixed rates, but if you stumble across one that will give you a fixed rate, you should consider in what direction the market is going before you make that decision.
- You will have to give your personal guarantee on the loan.
- Always stay one question ahead of the banker!
- Role-play on what you will give to the banker and what the banker will ask, accept.
- Consider taking out a side note. What I mean is if you still come up short after you have borrowed what you thought you needed to invest, you may have to use other sources of capital to fund the difference, i.e., an additional car loan, second mortgage, etc. These are what I call "side notes." With the first few real estate deals, I used this process effectively and put almost no out-of-pocket money into the deals or no money down.
- Equipment usually runs between seven- to ten-year amortization and real estate fifteen to twenty-five, but try to pay off in ten.

I would like to give you an example of thinking on your feet, and my personal experience with my first $500,000 loan at twenty-eight years of age. Trying to obtain my first loan was like pulling teeth, and you will find the experience about the same.

I had obtained a franchise for the Burger King in my area, which filled a void in the local market. I put together all the personal financials and started going to every bank in the city. Most of the bankers I talked to turned me down on the spot, but finally I went into the state's largest bank and met with the loan officer.

I had wanted to talk about myself and the experience I had, but he asked me several questions instead. He found out that I had gone to Mississippi State University and he was a huge football fan—and so was I. We discussed football for the next hour. I still knew a lot of players and I promised to get him a jersey from one of the quarterbacks that played in the Sun Bowl.

In the back of my mind, I was wondering if we were ever going to discuss the loan that I was requesting, which, by the way, was for the equipment to open the new Burger King only, and not for the real estate.

When I became a new Burger King franchisee, the Burger King Corporation would not allow franchisees to own the real estate on the first location. The primary reason was to allow them to terminate you as a franchisee if you were not a good operator.

I finally got up the nerve to ask if he would make the loan. To my surprise, he said he would make the loan, but there was one condition, a huge one. He and the bank would require a cosigner. My mind immediately started racing. I did not have a cosigner in mind when I approached the bank.

I started thinking about my dad, and I knew in my heart that he might consider cosigning the loan if I had a good plan. I already knew he had confidence in me because I had been working my fingers to the bone for the last ten years learning my profession.

So thinking quickly, my response to the banker was that I would get my dad to cosign for the first year only. I felt this would satisfy the bank, because usually most businesses fail within the first year. And, my dad was basically retired because of a bad heart problem, and I knew he would not want to have the liability hanging over him.

The banker agreed to the one-year cosign and I was off to meet with my father to plead for his signature. Needless to say, this was one of the biggest moments of my life. Facing my father and requesting his faith and signature was monumental.

I called and went over to discuss the situation with him in detail. His first response was that he was too old to be doing this and that he was basically retired. I told him that I only needed the cosign for one year and I would do everything humanly possible to keep his credit intact. He looked long and hard into my eyes and agreed to cosign.

That was the best gift I had ever received in my business life. I thanked my father, and the rest is history. From that point, I went on to develop fifteen to twenty restaurants over the next ten years.

NEGOTIATE EVERYTHING

You will need to remember this phrase: EVERYTHING IS NEGOTIABLE.

As you grow in your business, you will need to negotiate everything. You won't believe how much money this will save you over time. The goal here is always to seek out two or three quotes before you buy anything. I don't like to use the words *never* and *always*, but you must obtain quotes before you purchase anything. It would be a good idea to visit a bookstore and purchase books on this subject so that you can learn basic skills. They will be worth their weight in gold.

I know what you're thinking, *the lowest price is not always the best product*, but it is when you are talking about apples for apples, as the saying goes.

If it were the exact same product, why would you pay more? All those dollars saved will be tremendous at the end of the year.

When you are purchasing services such as phone, Internet, and so on, it's important to shop these also. Most people fall asleep and do not pay attention to what they are spending. Don't let that happen to you. Once you set up all the services you will need, go back every three years and see if there is a better mousetrap. You will be surprised at how many changes there will be and how you can improve your service and sometimes a better price to boot.

When you set up your financials, it's a good idea to look at all the line items and revisit them every three years. Another area of overlooked savings is usually your insurance—car, home, business general liability, property, casualty, and so on.

Fees are another area of potential savings. Banking fees are extremely expensive and usually you can negotiate those also. I personally like to pool all my funds into one account or sweep account and then pay all my bills online.

DETAILS + DETAILS + DETAILS = EXCELLENCE

Always pay attention to the details, and this will reward you with excellence. Don't let anything slide or take things for granted, because it will come back to haunt you. Even if you don't have the time that specific moment to address a situation, make a note of it and address it later.

I personally keep a little piece of paper and a pen in my pocket at all times. Usually, my best ideas on how to improve come while I am driving my car, watching sports, and other non-business activities; that's why it is important to make a note!

Make sure you thoroughly read all your contracts, including the fine print, before signing, and always be sure to strike out automatic renewals in contracts or service agreements, unless they roll over at a lower price. You can be assured that contract writers will usually raise the price, thinking you are not paying attention.

This really comes into play if you allow the vendor to renew automatically and you decide to sell your company. The new buyer may not accept or assume the contract; then you will have to buy it out, costing you thousands of dollars.

PERSONNEL

The most important advice I can give you regarding your staff is to always treat your staff as you would want to be treated. Once you grow into multiple locations, you will want to put a few systems in place to prevent one of your store or location managers from forgetting this valuable point.

Don't be greedy once you start making money; provide the best employee benefits that your particular industry warrants. Your employees will stay longer and become more loyal. Others in the community will want to work for your company, and eventually you will see lower turnover. Lower turnover will save you thousands of dollars in training wages, and keep experienced folks at the line level, making your job a lot easier.

My first experience with people skills came at the tender age of fifteen years old. My father was in the restaurant business and I started working there when I was twelve. Well, one summer, my father was remodeling a building out of town and left me behind every day to open the restaurant. We would ride together to work, pick up the help, and then I would set up and open the restaurant so he could go to his remodel project out of town.

Well, that particular morning, the night shift had left the restaurant a mess and I was taking it out on the morning crew. The next thing I knew, the entire staff told me to stick it where the sun doesn't shine and all of them walked out.

Needless to say, I really began to panic. I set the restaurant up for business first and then I began calling everyone I knew to come in, but I got no one.

Just by pure luck, my dad had forgotten something and he came back to the restaurant to pick it up. He noticed all the employees walking down the highway. He stopped, picked them up, and brought them back to the restaurant.

I can't tell you how relieved I was to see my dad walk in with the employees. My tail was tucked; he knew he didn't have to say anything to me because I had already beaten myself up over the ordeal.

From that point on, I always treated my staff with the utmost respect, did not take my frustrations out on them, always tried to look at both sides of a situation, and used as much professionalism as possible. Firm but fair became my mantra.

I would constantly ask my managers at monthly meetings to ask themselves what their staff would say about them if they died tomorrow.

How to be a good manager: SHBBB

1. Stay open
2. Have a sense of humor
3. Be honest
4. Be sincere
5. Be sensible

Remember these five points and you will be successful. If you ever do have to discipline an employee, you should remember these steps:

How to discipline an employee: CRISP

1. Consistent
2. Reasonable
3. Immediate
4. Specific
5. Personal

SYSTEMS IN PLACE

Once you get your company off the ground, it would be wise to set up systems in place...in writing.

First of all, what are systems in place? Every function in your company should have a written system in place for everything, such as personnel, payroll, accounting, cash procedures, vacations, profit sharing, 401k programs, and so on.

This will save you a tremendous amount of time when it comes to training new employees and in the general confusion that comes with not having a written plan in place. This will also help eliminate employee grievances in the future over specific details of your operations.

STUDY TIME

You will need to set aside a specific time of day to study and reflect to stay on top of your game. Personally, I spend about fifteen minutes first thing in the morning studying material, and even if I have read the same material one hundred times, I continue to study and eventually memorize the material. Be an expert!

Also, I spend another fifteen minutes thinking about what happened the previous day and how I could improve any issues or perform better.

ROLE MODEL

If possible, try to find someone in a similar business who excels at what he or she does and use him or her as your role model. Also, try to develop a relationship with this person and ask him or her for advice.

Personally, when I got my business off the ground, I sought out the best Burger King franchisee in the business. I called the man on the phone and he was more than happy to meet with me and give me great advice on all kinds of issues—how to structure an office staff, his organizational chart, systems in place, copies of handbooks, and so on.

OUTSOURCE PERSONNEL

Other than your direct labor to sell your product or service, it's a wise decision to outsource your accounting functions, that is, your financials, profit and loss statements, balance sheets, and payroll. There are a lot of companies that perform these services; be sure to get two to three quotes before committing.

TIME MANAGEMENT

At some point, once you become successful, your time will become very valuable to you; therefore, you must develop a system in place to manage your time.

If a nearby university offers a course or seminar, I highly recommend you attend one.

The system I used was the A B C method. Every day at the end of the day, I would religiously take a few minutes and write down what I was going to do tomorrow and prioritize the day. The As were must do, Bs were should do, and Cs were to do later. You would be amazed how on task this list will keep you and the tasks you will complete each day. I found this system to be invaluable and one I still use to this day.

STAYING CURRENT

Go to the bookstore periodically and seek out books that discuss the economy and where it's headed, management, marketing, and so on—anything that will give you a heads up on what's going on now and into the future.

Most of the time, the books will not be up to date, but they will give you a lot of ideas on how to better manage your business.

What I used to do was highlight the most important thoughts while I was reading so I could go back later to review the main points repeatedly.

If you get an opportunity, purchase a course in speed-reading. It is one of the best investments I have ever made. The simple concepts it teaches will allow you to read through large volumes of data and still comprehend the material. It gives you a different way to look at reading that will make you more productive and efficient. It's my understanding that most universities and smaller community colleges offer such courses.

TIMING

Timing is everything.

Over time, you will develop a good idea about when to perform certain functions or make certain purchases; for example, when to hire new employees, add new locations, start a new project, and so on, so that you will have no surprises in your business cycles and interruptions in your cash flow.

There are certain times of the year when your ideas will blend into your existing business or personal life cycles, and some of those will be better times than others. Be sure to take the time and evaluate the best time to perform a task that will have the least amount of negative impact on your current situation.

For example, the restaurant business is very cyclical. In the months of September, October, and until Thanksgiving in November, this period was always slow for us; therefore, we implemented sales programs to help deflect the slowdown. From Thanksgiving until the end of the year, sales were excellent with all the Christmas shopping going on. This was a good time to make money. Then, January and February would be slow because everyone spent most of their disposable income on Christmas gifts. In March, when all the income tax money starting flowing, sales picked back up and remained strong through the rest of the year until school started, as most people would spend their money on school supplies; then the cycle would start all over again.

With this knowledge, you could plan for most of your heavy expenditures to be during the highest sales months to maximize your cash flow.

Not only does this apply to your business life, but also to your personal life decisions; timing will affect every decision you make.

For example, I sold my business and 60 percent of my real estate holdings in August 2007 when the market was at its peak, therefore, maximizing my returns. It's all about timing.

Remember, the best surprise is no surprise. So, if you prepare for most everything that comes your way you will not have any bad surprises in your business decisions.

QUALITY PRODUCT

Whatever your product or service, be sure to deliver the best product for the price, and never substitute quality. The consumer will always want and command quality products and services, and pay the lowest price available. Check with Wal-Mart and see if this program has been successful for them. It's made them the number one retailer in the world. Every Wal-Mart in the United States or abroad has low-income as well as high-income consumers shop with them. Why? Price and Quality. QUALITY NEVER GOES OUT OF STYLE.

COMPLAINTS

The most important thing to remember when handling a complaint is to first empathize with the customer; in other words, defuse the situation. Then, you need to go all out to correct the situation, as it will be worth its weight in gold as far as future sales are concerned.

For example, if someone made a mistake by giving out a wrong sandwich or order, I would give the customer a free meal the next time he or she came in. By taking care of the meal how much did it really cost? I know what you are thinking. *The customer will make a habit of it and the cost will be too high.* Let's take a closer look at the cost for a moment.

The actual cost for a hamburger, fries, and a Coke, or what you may know as a value meal, is actually about $1.45; the retail price would be about $4.59. This particular customer is a regular customer and frequents the restaurant about three times a week for a total of $13.77, or $716.04 a year, and you are reluctant to give back the $1.45 in free food for the mistake *you* made.

This is a classic example of being penny-wise and pound-foolish. You can see the consequences of your decision in real numbers.

If you are going to be in retail or any other profession, then you have to go the extra mile to satisfy your customers. Trust me, they will remember!

In other words, EXCEED THE CUSTOMERS EXPECTATIONS!

For example, one day for lunch, while I was working the drive-through window, I put the wrong sandwich in this particular woman's bag. She worked at the hospital and had only thirty minutes for lunch. When she got back to the hospital, she realized the mistake I had made and called me on the phone. I apologized promptly, made sure I had the correct sandwich, found out the address of her business, and I personally hand delivered the entire order right to her at her desk at the hospital.

In addition, I gave her a coupon for a free complete meal on her next visit.

In other words, I exceeded every expectation she could ever imagine and that's what you will need to do. She could not believe the extra effort and I can't tell you how many people came up to me and asked me if I had actually done that. She told everyone at the hospital how wonderful we were and what a wonderful experience she had. Remember, I took a bad situation and turned it around.

We won a loyal and dedicated customer for life. She still recalls the incident to this day and brags about it.

EXCEED the customer's expectations and you will win the competitive battle in your town or area.

FREE PAIR OF EYES

Sometimes customers would call me at home when I would be off from work and while I had friends or company over. A guest would say, "I bet you hate to get those calls at home, don't you," and I would respond quite the opposite. If a customer calls me at home, then I would sincerely appreciate the call because I was getting a FREE PAIR OF EYES, in other words, a watchdog for free while I'm not at the job site.

Therefore, I would use those calls as a good source to find out exactly what happened, when it happened, who was on duty when it happened, and so on.

Then, I would use the information to improve my business for free. Be sure never to reveal your source or free employee watchdog.

What a great way to benefit your company at someone else's expense. I would tell all my customers to call with any issues they may have. In the end, numerous free pairs of eyes, or watchdogs, aided me.

MAJOR IN MAJORS

I had a controller name Judy who worked for me for twenty years. She used to say to me, all the time to "major in majors and not in minors."

Her point was what the first part of this book is all about—planning and majors. Like me, you all can relate to sometimes, getting caught up in all the daily things in life (minors) can be an obstacle in focusing on your majors. Yes, all the minors of the day have to be done, but don't forget the Big Picture.

Your daily "to do" list will help protect you from this phenomenon, and once you build your staff and personnel, you can delegate the minors so that you may have more time to devote to your majors.

POINT OF SALE SYSTEMS

If you decide to go into retail and you develop multiple locations, then you will need to have a standardized point of sale system in all your locations. Point of sale systems are the cash registers that you will need to check out your customers.

It's important to have all your systems the same so that you can send someone to help out at another location and he or she will know how to operate the system. It's also important for inventory control.

At some point, you will begin polling data from all your locations, and a standardized system will allow you to do this. It will keep you up to date on all your sales and help you know what inventory is moving and what is not. You will also want to poll your locations daily to report sales. By doing this, you can use the sales data to pool your cash and better manage your cash flow.

A good point of sale system can give you all kinds of valuable data about your business—average check, sales for the day; units sold of each product; labor reporting; sales for the week, month, and year; customer counts; inventory counts; waste; speed of service or transaction times; and other factors.

GOVERNMENT ASSISTANCE PROGRAMS

Did you know that the federal government has several programs to help you if you want to take advantage of them?

If you need to borrow money, I would suggest you go to the Small Business Administration, or SBA; they will assist you in purchasing equipment or real estate for your first venture if you cannot locate funds from local banks.

The federal government will also give you tax credits for existing employees if you meet certain criteria. These are really attractive if you live in or locate your business in an empowerment zone. The program is called the Work Opportunity Tax Credit and it will pay you to train new employees.

These programs can really make a difference for you and help you be successful: SBA Loan Program, empowerment zone, and Work Opportunity Tax Credit.

Go online and become familiar with these programs.

MAXIMIZE YOUR RETURNS WHENEVER AND WHEREVER YOU POSSIBLY CAN:

EMPLOYEE BONUSES AND PROFIT SHARING

Earlier in the book, I laid out a Wheel of Success for the Best Company on Earth. Well, you won't get there unless every employee in your company is behind you 100 percent. The best way to motivate employees, I have found, is with money.

Not only should you pay your employees the highest average hourly rate in town, also consider allowing your crew to earn monthly bonuses, which will set your staff on fire.

For example, I had a mystery shopper who would rank my quality, service, and cleanliness on a monthly basis. Based on that score, each employee would receive $5, $10, or $20 extra in his or her paycheck.

Managers would receive bonuses on food cost, labor, and sales increases.

We had specific guidelines, but in general, managers could receive at least $500 dollars monthly in each category, or a total of $1,500 monthly if they maxed out the program. The district managers would receive 25 percent of what the managers earned.

Having everyone tied into the future success of each other is a powerful stimulator, and they will tell everyone in the community, which will actually help with recruiting future employees.

I also had a profit-sharing program for every employee, down to each crew-level person. I did not ask anyone to contribute to the plan. I contributed monies into their account monthly, depending on an allowable amount set by the IRS and the profitability of our company.

One word of caution, however; you have measurable ways to define the criteria for giving bonuses. ALL SUCCESS MUST BE MEASURED. This can be done through financial statements and mystery shopper programs.

Part 6
Purchasing Real Estate

As I mentioned earlier, I was a Burger King franchisee for twenty-three years. I was able to accumulate a significant amount of money by being an expert in operations. But if you remember, I mentioned buying and controlling real estate on each new location that I built.

Over the years, I developed several points that I would always use when I was seeking out those new sites. I understand not everyone who reads this book is in the retail side of things, but most of my thoughts will apply to everyone.

If you are not comfortable with seeking out your own locations or do not have any experience, then it might be a good idea to seek out a local commercial real estate agent who can assist you. If you are buying a national franchise, they may have an internal real estate department to help you secure your site.

What to look for in a great location:

First, you will need to identify who your retail customer is and try to make your location as accessible as possible. The typical Burger King customer is usually eighteen to forty-nine years old and frequents a fast-food restaurant about seven times a week.

You can go to the government site www.cencus.gov to obtain a significant amount of demographic information so you can be sure the area or town has enough people and disposable income to support your new location.

The population should be at least twenty thousand and the disposable income should be $15,000 annually. You can buy demographic reports for this information, but I suggest obtaining them for free from the above site because it's where reporting agencies would find the information and sell it to you.

Then, call all the local developers in the area and see what new developments are being considered or are about to start. Usually, someone will have an outparcel to sell if they are going to construct a Wal-Mart strip center or large shopping center, for example. A site next to the new Wal-Mart in town is always a good choice. It's a good idea to develop a relationship with the Wal-Mart Corporation real estate person who is in charge of your area, so that if they are considering building a new center and have an existing one, you will know about the change ahead of time. The area where the old one is will take a significant loss in revenue for the area, especially if it is a small town. Wal-Mart draws about six thousand to ten thousand cars a day. Don't build your new retail site on the wrong side of town. You need to find out what will be happening in the next five to ten years in the area.

You can also go down to the building permit office where you reside and obtain a list of all new permits and future permits.

Contact the department of transportation for the state in which you live and let them know what your plans are and that you are trying to identify the best area to locate a new business. Ask for the ten-year plan, and be sure to have a good understanding of this map. You want to find this out because it will give you an idea of where new traffic is going and if the state or county is looking into widening a road in front of the new location you are thinking about purchasing.

Car traffic counts are an important step in this process also and should be obtained from the state in which you reside. The higher the traffic count, the better, but the downside to a busy area is whether a person can navigate into the site easily. Be sure to look for this.

If you know who your competitors are, you need to locate them on a map, and when you drive by them (the market), make a note of where they are and why you think they are located there.

Mark on your map all the main north, south, east and west corridors or roads before driving the market in your car.

Now, let's recap the highlights:

1. Obtain demographics from a census Web site
2. Call local developers
3. Check with Wal-Mart
4. Obtain information from the state or county about traffic count, the ten-year plan, road widening, etc.
5. Collect building permits from the local government
6. Obtain city and state maps
7.   Locate competition on map
8. Mark main streets: north, south, east, and west

Now, it's time to ride the market in your car so you can get down to the street level. And, if you can afford the expense, a plane ride over the area would give a tremendous bird's eye view.

There is no substitute for driving the market in your car, but I would also go to the Internet and seek out the tax assessor's office in the area to get ownership maps and aerials that would show all the property and vacant land from the air. I found these to be invaluable.

A good retail location will have a good amount of office space close by, homes and apartments, and retail stores such as

Wal-Mart, Stein Mart, Lowe's, Home Depot, and so on; you need all three.

Try to find a corner lot that is on the right side of the road. This is because a customer would be able to make a right-hand turn into your property; having a traffic light to regulate traffic is another plus.

Also, you want to be sure that a customer coming in the opposite direction can easily make a left-hand turn into your property. Many people do not consider this important element. The customer has to have access to your site from both directions to maximize your potential sales at the location.

I like to check the tags in major shopping centers to confirm where the sales traffic is coming from. Many states' tags include the county in which the owner resides. This information is vital because it gives you an idea as to what is happening in the area and who is frequenting businesses near your potential location.

In summary, you want a site that has high visibility, excellent traffic counts, access from both directions, a traffic light, good demographics, a low crime rate, is a corner lot, is a pad site (vacant lot in front of large shopping center) of a major retailer, and is in a new area of town.

In most cases, you will not be able to secure all these items, but try to obtain as many as possible. Usually, the price will be higher for these types of locations. I would recommend paying a higher price for a primary location rather than buying a location in a secondary site.

For instance, if the primary site is $800,000 and the secondary is $500,000, you should always purchase the primary site, because you would be financing the property anyway, and the $300,000 difference will be amortized over the life of the loan. And, if you secure a fifteen-year loan then $300,000 over the life of the loan is not a deal breaker. The extra money spent on the primary site versus the secondary site will reward you in extra sales and help out-position your competition.

If your career takes you down a path where you cannot own real estate as a passive investment, then you will need to invest in real estate from the profits of your operating company.

Some good real estate investments are commercial properties; that is, single-tenant retail with absolute net leases, strip centers with multiple tenants with triple net leases, or foreclosed commercial properties. Just be sure they are income producing and not vacant. If you don't have the time to manage the property yourself, then for a 3 to 5 percent fee, there are real estate companies that will perform the management function for you.

Don't forget, if commercial is not your thing, you can buy residential property or foreclosed homes and rent them out.

The point is to have passive income!

Part 7
Marketing Tips for
Television and Radio

When the operations of your company reach the point where you can advertise, consider these points.

First, representatives of all radio stations and television stations will tell you that they have the number one station in town. The way to be sure is to obtain a copy of an Arbitron report, which will tell you who is really best in your area. These reports can be expensive, so try to find a local person in the area who will share with you or at least help with the cost of the report. If you are a national chain franchisee, then the franchisor may assist.

For radio, you will want to advertise during drive times, 6:00 a.m. to 9:00 a.m. and 3:00 p.m. to 6:00 p.m., and negotiate a yearly contract and payment for random programming or regular rotation.

For television, you will need at least 300 Gross Rating Points (each television program is measured by how many viewers watch a program and will be rated with points) to reach your audience, and the local news is always a great spot to purchase. I spent most of my advertising dollars on TV, because with TV, you receive SIGHT, SOUND, and MOTION, which are very powerful.

I did not purchase newspaper or other print ads very often, and they are my least favorite.

As a rule, I spent 75 percent of my advertising on TV and 25 percent on radio.

Part 8
Maintain the Wealth

The best advice I could give you once you have this plan solidly in place is to consider where to park your money, and that place is Vanguard. That's one of the best decisions I made. How do you invest your money at Vanguard? If you have enough funds, you can use the advice of Vanguard for a small fee. Otherwise, you can invest your money into only two funds.

Invest 50 to 60 percent in the World Fund and 40 to 50 percent in the Total Bond Fund or Intermediate Muni Fund if taxes are a problem. Then, once or twice a year, sell off one or the other fund to bring the percentages back to your goals.

It's very important to do this because, ultimately, you are selling stocks when they get overheated and moving to the safety of bonds, and vice versa when bonds are high and stocks are undervalued.

The main idea to take from this is to stay the course no matter what the market is doing—and turn the TV off.

Don't buy individual stocks or day trade.

Don't start buying other businesses.

Just because you are successful, that does not make you an expert in another field.

If you generate excess cash, then immediately go to the bank and pay off some of your real estate notes.

As the years go by, the next big decisions will be to sell your business and real estate or pass it along to family. Remember you have two companies at this point; one owns and operates the business and the other owns the real estate.

My dad always used to tell me that the economy runs in ten-year cycles. The first few years would be difficult and the following years would be OK, until it recycled again. What I found out was that, sometimes, the bad years would start early in the decade or come later into the decade. Therefore, it's only a guide and not set in stone.

But you can rest assured, when the economy becomes weak that's the ideal time to borrow money and to construct facilities, because everyone is looking for new business.

Part 9
Giving Back

Once your business and career are successful, at some point, you will need to give back to the community that has been so kind to you. I have always felt that with children, you have the best opportunity to be impactful on their lives at an earlier stage in life versus later, because you have more of a chance to change behavior.

I believe it's easier to influence children than change the behavior of an adult. Usually, it's too late with adults, but working and mentoring kids is a great way to give back to the community.

I donate to schools, support reading programs, give speeches, and mentor; also, I founded the Burger King Academy for an elementary school.

Helping kids can be very rewarding.

I would also recommend being involved in your church. As a Catholic my entire life, I have been active in my church and am a former board member of the finance council. I usually don't like to discuss religion and politics, and I would highly recommend you to stay neutral with all your customers when those two topics come up.

I am a devout Catholic, but I do not push my thoughts on anyone with regard to church and politics. My feelings are for myself and myself only.

I will say one important statistical fact about the Catholic Appeal Services. For every dollar you give, you receive $7 in service, and I love to get the most for my dollars. This is really an incredible fact, because in most other charities, the most that goes to the service or people that need the services is twenty to thirty cents on the dollar, and everything else goes to administration costs.

Most people are very emotional with regard to these two issues and, therefore, in my opinion, I would just be a good listener.

I mention God just to let you know it is important to me to have God in my life. I can't tell you how many times a major decision has come up such that if I went in one direction, the outcome would be fantastic and rewarding financially, but if I went the other way, there would be a significant loss of capital.

I would make decisions that sometimes seemed as if someone upstairs must have guided me in the right direction, because the results were successful.

Having God in your life is a good thing and I will leave that with you.

Part 10
Possible Future Careers

Looking back, I can think of a couple of vocations that would be good career choices for students of the future—financial planner, money manager, mutual fund manager, bank trust manager, and so on, or any position dealing with the management of money. These are smart careers, because the population is getting older and people will need help managing their monies. These careers can be rewarding because you would get an opportunity to help people, and you don't have to be great at it. Did you know that most mutual fund managers make millions but cannot beat the Standard and Poor average in the stock market?

Where else can you make that much money and be average? Another profession worth taking a look at is being a general contractor. The reason I say this is because the federal government has a program that people will not tell you about, and it's one of those things you find out later in life and say you wish you had known about that.

HUD, the U.S. Department of Housing and Urban Development, offers the program. Through this program, the federal government will allow you to build apartment complexes if you are a licensed general contractor and they will give you a non-recourse loan, which means you do not have to pay the money back if your venture fails. They will require no money down, as long as when you build the project you let your 15 to 20 percent contractor's markup go into the property. Through this program, the government will allow you to build a ninety- to two-hundred-plus-unit apartment complex. The federal government does this nationwide to provide housing to those who cannot afford to purchase homes of their own.

I personally know someone who did this for twenty years and accumulated five thousand apartment units, which he just recently sold for millions.

Part 11
Final Thoughts and Recap

During the course of your business career, you will obviously have days that are better than others. When you catch a tough day, this is what I used to say to my personnel:

NEVER GET UPSET. ALWAYS KEEP YOUR COOL AND POISE UNDER ALL CONDITIONS, BECAUSE WHEN YOU ARE OUT OF CONTROL, SOMEONE ELSE IS IN CONTROL.

I understand starting out in your career or starting a new business will look and feel like a monumental task, but it's all about how you look at it.

I always look at everything like a piece or block of Swiss cheese—you know, the kind with all the holes in it. I look at each hole as a process to get to the next hole in the cheese. I start with the lower holes and keep moving till I get to the top. This mental process keeps me from getting frustrated and giving up. You will need to develop your own thoughts to keep you on track.

You may reach me at my e-mail address if you have any questions or need further explanation of any of the comments in this book. harry@noblefs.com.

Part 12
Recipe for a Good Day

1. LARGE CUP OF JOY
2. PINCH OF HAPPINESS
3. ONE POUND OF LAUGHTER
4. TEASPOON OF SILLINESS
5. MIX WELL AND BAKE AT 350 DEGREES FOR TEN MINUTES
6. MAKES ONE FULL DAY OF FUN!